Shea, Robert Kennedy   799.2
The Great Outdoors: Hunting   SHE

	DATE DUE		
2/11/16			

THE GREAT OUTDOORS
HUNTING

By Robert Kennedy Shea

Gareth Stevens
Publishing

Please visit our website, www.garethstevens.com. For a free color catalog of all our high-quality books, call toll free 1-800-542-2595 or fax 1-877-542-2596.

Library of Congress Cataloging-in-Publication Data

Shea, Robert Kennedy.
Hunting / Robert Kennedy Shea.
    p. cm. — (The great outdoors)
Includes index.
ISBN 978-1-4339-7100-6 (pbk.)
ISBN 978-1-4339-7101-3 (6-pack)
ISBN 978-1-4339-7099-3 (library binding)
1. Hunting—Juvenile literature. I. Title.
SK35.5.S54 2013
799.2—dc23

                                             2011051099

First Edition

Published in 2013 by
Gareth Stevens Publishing
111 East 14th Street, Suite 349
New York, NY 10003

Copyright © 2013 Gareth Stevens Publishing

Designer: Michael J. Flynn
Editor: Therese Shea

Photo credits: Cover, p. 1 Rubberball Productions/The Agency Collection/Getty Images; pp. 5, 8, 18 Bruce MacQueen/Shutterstock.com; p. 6 iStockphoto.com/Jon Huelskamp; p. 9 jarobike/Shutterstock.com; p. 10 iStockphoto.com/NanoStock; p. 10 Peter Gyure/ Shutterstock.com; p. 13 (main) Guy J. Sagi/Shutterstock.com; p. 13 (inset) Nekrasov Audrey/Shutterstock.com; p. 14 iStockphoto.com/beachnet; p. 16 PHB.cz (richard Semik)/ Shutterstock.com; p. 17 Barna Tanko/Shutterstock.com; p. 21 Spencer Pratt/Getty Images.

Printed in the United States of America

CPSIA compliance information: Batch #CS12GS: For further information contact Gareth Stevens, New York, New York at 1-800-542-2595.

CONTENTS

Man vs. Nature 4

License to Hunt 7

Deer Hunting 8

Bird Hunting 11

Hunting Calls 12

Types of Weapons 15

Hunting Dogs 16

Hunting Laws 18

To Hunt or Not to Hunt 20

Glossary 22

For More Information 23

Index 24

Words in the glossary appear in **bold** type the first time they are used in the text.

MAN VS. NATURE

Can you imagine being really hungry, but having to find your food in the wild rather than buy it? People once had to do that. If they wanted some fruit, they had to pick it. If they wanted fish, they had to catch it. And if they wanted meat, they had to hunt.

Today, most Americans don't have to hunt for food. However, many hunt for sport and for the satisfaction of capturing their own food. Hunters enjoy being in nature and trying to outsmart an animal.

INTO THE WILD

Many animals, such as deer, have excellent senses of smell and hearing. They know if a person is nearby.

4

Hunters have **weapons**, but animals are quicker than people and have sharper senses.

5

About 16 million people buy hunting **licenses** each year in the United States.

U.S.
RESERVATION
BOUNDARY
MARK
DO NOT
DISTURB

PUBLIC
HUNTING

6

LICENSE TO HUNT

People hunt all kinds of animals: turkeys, ducks, deer, bears, and even squirrels. But they can't hunt whenever they want. They need a license from the government. There are different kinds of licenses depending on the weapons a hunter uses.

Most states require a hunter to take a safety course. There's usually an age requirement as well, but young hunters may be able to get a junior hunting license. Hunting can be dangerous, so it's important that all hunters are well trained.

INTO THE WILD

DEER HUNTING

Game is any animal hunted for food or sport. In North America, big game includes moose and bears, but the most popular is deer.

Some hunters follow, or stalk, deer. However, it's hard to sneak up on a deer, so hunters may build a tree stand and wait in it for a deer to pass by. A blind is a hiding place on the ground for the same purpose. Sometimes hunters work together and chase deer toward each other.

INTO THE WILD

Although the practice is illegal in many places, some hunters use bait, such as corn and oats, to draw game to them.

Hunters place tree stands and blinds in areas where deer are known to feed, such as fields.

duck decoy

Birds that swim in the water are called waterfowl.

BIRD HUNTING

Bird hunters use many methods to get their game. Duck or goose hunters may put fake birds called decoys on the water to draw real birds to them. Then they wait in a boat or hide in a blind nearby.

Other kinds of bird hunting include **quail**, **pheasant**, and turkey hunting. Some people have **preserves** on which they raise these birds for the purpose of hunting. But bird hunters can find places to hunt on public land, too.

INTO THE WILD

Hunters should wear bright orange clothing so other hunters won't mistake them for game. It's a law in some places.

11

HUNTING CALLS

It's almost impossible to stalk a turkey. Turkey hunters can draw the birds to them by making a sound like a turkey looking for a **mate**. Duck hunters make sounds like ducks so their decoys seem even more real to real ducks. Big-game hunters may call out like a wounded animal so another animal comes looking for a meal.

Some hunters make these calls using their own voice. Others use special **devices**. Electronic hunting calls are illegal in many places because they're considered to be unfair to the animals.

INTO THE WILD

The National Wild Turkey Federation holds the Grand National Calling Contest each year. Hunters who make the best turkey calls can win prizes.

12

duck calls

turkey call

Hunters today use many kinds of devices to make hunting calls. For thousands of years, Native Americans used turkey wing bones!

Some hunters prefer to hunt with bows and crossbows rather than guns. These are just as dangerous as guns.

TYPES OF WEAPONS

Hunters use different types of weapons. **Rifles** are used to shoot both big and small game from far away. However, many places don't allow rifle hunting because the **ammunition** can travel beyond the hunting area.

Shotguns are used for closer game. **Birdshot** spreads as it's fired, making it easier to hit a small moving animal. Buckshot shells contain larger pieces for hitting larger game. A slug is a solid chunk of metal ammunition. "Rifled" slugs are grooved so they spin in a shotgun, resulting in a long and exact shot.

INTO THE WILD

HUNTING DOGS

Some people use dogs when they hunt. Bird dogs are trained to locate a bird after a hunter has shot it down. Pointers are good bird dogs. When a pointer smells a bird, it points with its body in the direction of the game.

Hounds, such as beagles and greyhounds, are another kind of hunting dog. Some hounds are taught to follow game by sight, while others have an excellent sense of smell. Retrievers are trained to find and bring back, or retrieve, game such as waterfowl.

This Pudelpointer uses its body to show its owner where a bird fell.

17

HUNTING LAWS

There are many laws to follow when hunting. Some laws are meant to help animals. They name what animals can be hunted, when and where they can be hunted, and the number that may be killed. Some animals can only be hunted with a special kind of license.

Many rules of hunting are meant to keep people safe. Hunting accidents can often be avoided. Hunters should always check with their local government for new laws and notices before they hunt.

Hunters are often not allowed to hunt animals during times of the year when the animals are having babies or raising their young.

HUNTING LAWS
CAUSE AND EFFECT

cause	law	effect
Some animals were hunted until they died out.	Hunters can only hunt certain animals at certain times.	Animals are able to mate and raise families.
Hunters harm other hunters by accident.	Hunters must wear orange clothing in many places.	Fewer hunting accidents take place.
People hurt themselves and others while hunting.	Hunters complete a safety course in order to get a license.	Hunters are less likely to harm others.

TO HUNT OR NOT TO HUNT

Some people oppose hunting. They believe hunting is cruel. They also worry people will change the balance of nature. In the past, before laws were put in place, some animals were hunted to **extinction**.

However, hunting also helps control animal populations. For example, large groups of deer can harm crops and spread illness. Some deer die of hunger because there's not enough food for all of them. As for cruelty, hunters try to kill with one shot to cause game as little pain as possible. Most hunters truly respect nature and wildlife.

HELP **STOP** THE NEW JERSEY BEAR HUNT!

MR. GOVERNOR!

STOP BEAR HUNT

STOP THE BEAR HUNT!

Many people have a strong opinion about hunting. What's your opinion?

GLOSSARY

ammunition: bullets, shells, and other things fired by weapons

birdshot: little balls of metal meant to be fired from a shotgun

device: a tool or machine built to perform a task

extinction: the death of all members of a kind of living thing

license: official permission from the government to do something

mate: one of two animals that come together to make babies. Also, to come together to make babies.

pheasant: a large bird related to chickens. Males are brightly colored and have long, curved tails.

preserve: a large area of land where animals are kept for their safety or to be hunted for sport

quail: a small bird with a round body, brown feathers, and a short tail

rifle: a gun with a long, grooved barrel that is fired from the shoulder

shotgun: a gun often used to fire a load of metal balls a short distance

weapon: something used to cause someone or something injury or death

FOR MORE INFORMATION

BOOKS

Klein, Adam G. *Hunting*. Edina, MN: ABDO Publishing, 2008.

Lundgren, Julie K. *Hunting*. Vero Beach, FL: Rourke, 2010.

WEBSITES

How Hunting Calls Work

adventure.howstuffworks.com/outdoor-activities/hunting/traditional-methods/hunting-call.htm

Read more about different kinds of hunting calls and hear what they sound like.

Hunting Safety

www.dec.ny.gov/outdoor/9186.html

Read about hunter safety and the best clothing to wear when deer hunting.

National Hunting and Fishing Day

www.nhfday.org

Learn about National Hunting and Fishing Day.

INDEX

bait 8

bears 7, 8

bird dogs 16

blind 8, 9, 11

bows 14

crossbows 14

decoys 10, 11, 12

deer 4, 7, 8, 9, 20

ducks 7, 10, 11, 12, 13

falconry 15

food 4, 8, 20

game 8, 11, 15, 16, 20

goose 11

guns 14, 15

hounds 16

hunting calls 12, 13

laws 18, 19, 20

license 6, 7, 18, 19

moose 8

oppose hunting 20

orange clothing 11, 19

pheasant 11

pointers 16, 17

quail 11

retrievers 16

rifles 15

safety 7, 19

shotguns 15

sport 4, 8

squirrels 7

tree stand 8, 9

turkeys 7, 11, 12, 13

weapons 5, 7, 15